Myths and Civilization of the

VIKINGS

Copyright © 1998 by McRae Books Srl, Florence, Italy

Published by
Peter Bedrick Books, Inc.
156 Fifth Avenue
New York, N.Y. 10010

The Myths & Civilization series
was created and produced by McRae Books,
via de' Rustici, 5 – Florence, Italy
Text Hazel Mary Martell
Editing Anne McRae, Mollie Thomson
Illustrations Francesca D'Ottavi (myths),
Ivan Stalio, Alessandro Cantucci, Andrea Morandi (civilization)
Graphic Design Marco Nardi
Cutouts Adriano Nardi, Ornella Fassio
Color separations R.A.F., Florence (Italy)

Printed and bound in Italy
by Grafiche Editoriali Padane, Cremona

00 99 98   1   2   3   4
First edition 1998
ISBN 0 87226 285 5

Myths and Civilization of the

VIKINGS

Hazel Mary Martell

Illustrated by
Francesca D'Ottavi & Ivan Stalio
Alessandro Cantucci & Andrea Morandi

PETER BEDRICK BOOKS
NEW YORK

CONTENTS

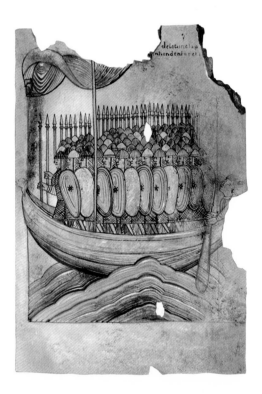

INTRODUCTION

The Vikings burst onto the stage of European history at the end of the 8th century with the first of a series of devastating raids on Britain and continental Europe. Lasting around 300 years (AD 800–1100), the Viking Age was spectacular and had enormous impact. The Vikings were a restless and daring people; from their rugged homelands in Norway, Denmark, and Sweden they explored Europe, setting up trade links with the Asian, Arab, and North African peoples on its eastern and southern fringes. They also traveled west, raiding and settling in England, Iceland, Greenland, and even North America, a good 500 years before Columbus! The Viking Age had faded by the 13th century, as the coming of Christianity changed Scandinavian society, but its rich heritage continues to the present-day.

HOW THIS BOOK WORKS

The book is divided into sections. Each one starts with a Viking myth, strikingly illustrated on a black background, followed by a non-fiction spread with information about Viking society. The last spread explains why the Viking civilization ended and what it has left us.

Spread with myth and illustration of the Valkyries leads on to a spread about Viking warriors and warfare.

The Vikings left behind them a rich store of myth and legend as well as a wealth of archeological evidence showing us how they lived their daily lives. In a unique approach, this book combines the two sources of information. By reading a myth in conjunction with history we allow the Vikings to explain themselves on their own terms before zooming in to look in more detail at how they really lived. History comes alive as we participate, for example, in the Vikings' battles and then examine their weapons, armor, and tactics.

THE BIRTH OF THE WORLD

The Vikings believed that the earth was created out of a great empty space called Ginnungagap. To the north of Ginnungagap lay the icy realm of Niflheim, while to the south was Muspell, which was made from flames and fire. Then Ginnungagap was slowly filled with ice from Niflheim. As the ice got nearer to Muspell it began to melt and two creatures were formed out of it. One was Ymir, the first Frost Giant, and the other was Audumla, a giant cow. She lived by licking the ice and Ymir fed on her milk. While Ymir lay sleeping, more Frost Giants and Giantesses grew out of his sweat.

One day Audumla found a huge, humanlike figure when she was licking the ice. She freed it from the ice and it turned into Buri. He later had a son called Bor. In his turn, Bor had three sons who became the first gods. Their names were Odin, Vili, and Ve. The gods hated the Frost Giants because they were harsh and cruel. They killed Ymir and made the world out of his body, using his flesh for the earth and his bones and teeth for the mountains and rocks. His blood was used for the seas and rivers and his skull was made into the dome of the sky, while his brain became the clouds. Bright sparks of fire from Muspell were then tossed into the sky to make the sun and moon, and the stars and planets.

After this, Odin, Vili, and Ve shaped the first humans from the roots of an ash tree and an elm tree which they found on the seashore. They called the man Ask because he was made from the ash tree, while the woman was called Embla because she was made from the elm. The gods breathed life into Ask and Embla and they became the ancestors of all humans. Around the same time, Odin, Vili, and Ve made the dwarfs from maggots that had crawled out of Ymir's flesh and gave four of them the task of holding up the sky.

Nothing more is heard of Vili and Ve, but Odin became the most important of all the gods and goddesses. From his home in Asgard he could see into the future and knew what fate held in store for everyone. He also knew everything that happened in the Nine Realms which made up the world and often traveled in disguise from one realm to another.

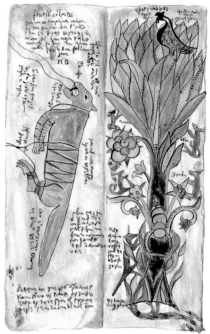

Religion and Burials

The Vikings believed in many different gods and goddesses. Some gods, such as Odin and Thor, are well known to us because many myths about them have survived. Others are less well known, and their roles and personalities have been lost. The Vikings also believed in life after death. Even the poorest of them were buried with some of their possessions, as well as food and drink, in preparation for their journey to the afterlife. Because they thought that this journey would be over water, many wealthy Vikings had themselves buried in a ship. Others were buried in graves marked out with stones in the shape of a ship.

The giant wolf Fenrir was an enemy of the gods, who kept him bound in chains. But at Ragnarök, the end of the world, the Vikings believed that he would break his chains and devour Odin. Fenrir is shown here in an Icelandic manuscript next to the sacred ash tree, Yggdrasil.

The Vikings sometimes sacrificed people on funeral pyres. This was done so that the dead person would have someone to help in their life after death. They were not the first inhabitants of Scandinavia to sacrifice people. This well-preserved body of a man was found by peat-cutters in Tollund Bog, Denmark, in 1950. He had been ceremonially strangled about 2000 years earlier.

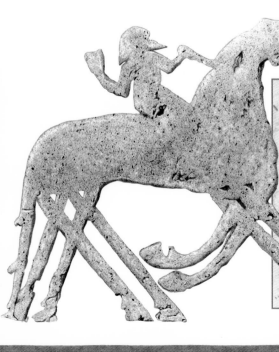

A VIKING FUNERAL
In 922, the Arab ambassador Ibn Fadlan watched the funeral of a Viking chief on the banks of the River Volga: "They brought a bier which was placed in the ship; they covered it with Byzantine brocade tapestries and with cushions... they brought fruit and sweet-smelling herbs and laid these beside him." A girl was led to the boat and killed so that she could look after him: "They laid her by the side of her dead master...." Then the ship was set on fire: "Soon it was burning brightly – first the boat, then the tent and the man and the maiden and everything in the boat." The ashes were later buried in a grave mound.

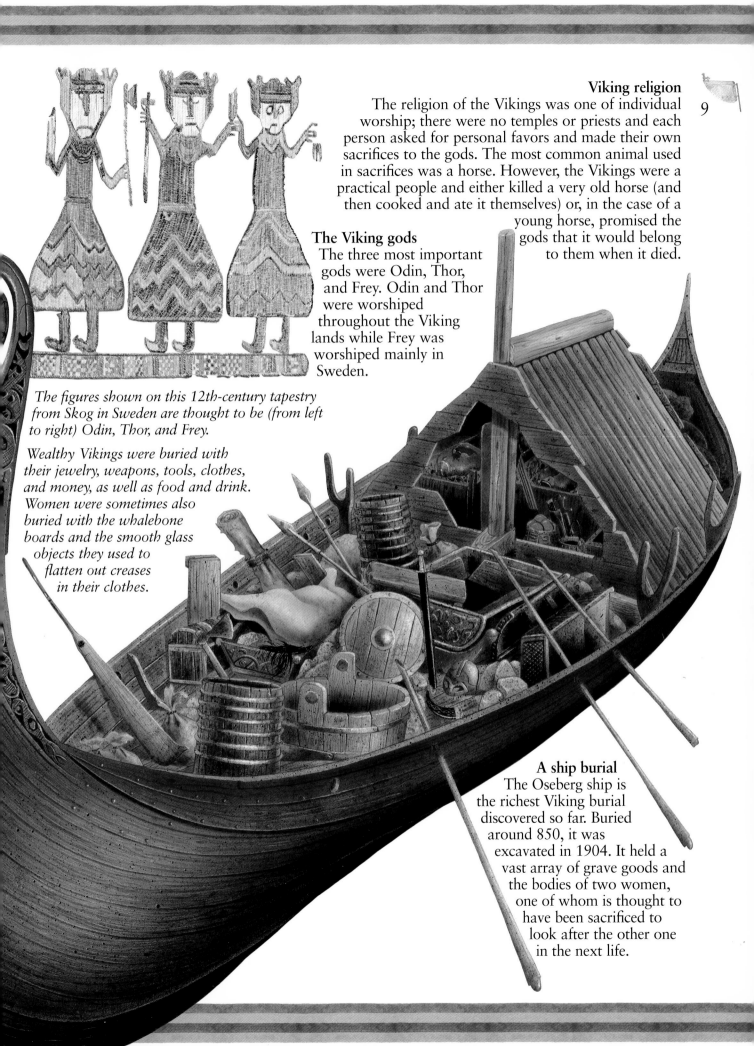

Viking religion

The religion of the Vikings was one of individual worship; there were no temples or priests and each person asked for personal favors and made their own sacrifices to the gods. The most common animal used in sacrifices was a horse. However, the Vikings were a practical people and either killed a very old horse (and then cooked and ate it themselves) or, in the case of a young horse, promised the gods that it would belong to them when it died.

The Viking gods

The three most important gods were Odin, Thor, and Frey. Odin and Thor were worshiped throughout the Viking lands while Frey was worshiped mainly in Sweden.

The figures shown on this 12th-century tapestry from Skog in Sweden are thought to be (from left to right) Odin, Thor, and Frey.

Wealthy Vikings were buried with their jewelry, weapons, tools, clothes, and money, as well as food and drink. Women were sometimes also buried with the whalebone boards and the smooth glass objects they used to flatten out creases in their clothes.

A ship burial

The Oseberg ship is the richest Viking burial discovered so far. Buried around 850, it was excavated in 1904. It held a vast array of grave goods and the bodies of two women, one of whom is thought to have been sacrificed to look after the other one in the next life.

HEIMDALL AND HUMAN SOCIETY

One day Heimdall decided to visit Midgard. Disguised as a man and calling himself Rig, he first went to the home of a poor man and his wife. Their names were Ai and Edda and their tiny house was built from blocks of turf. However, when Rig knocked on the door and asked for food and shelter, they welcomed him in and shared their coarse bread and simple stew with him. Rig stayed with Ai and Edda for three nights and repaid their kindness by causing the childless Edda to have a son. He was named Thrall, meaning slave, and in due course he married a woman called Bondmaid and they became the ancestors of all future thralls.

Rig went next to a prosperous-looking farm, owned by Alf and his childless wife, Amma. When he asked them for food and shelter, they also welcomed him in and fed him on calf-stew and other tasty foods. Again he stayed for three nights and repaid their kindness by causing Amma to have a son. This son was called Karl, meaning freeman. In due course he also married and had children. He and his wife became the ancestors of all future karls.

Finally Rig went to a great hall where wealthy Fathir and his childless wife, Mothir, lived. Again Rig asked for food and shelter and here he was entertained with the very best of everything. He stayed for three nights and repaid Fathir and Mothir's kindness by causing her to have a son too. His name was Jarl, meaning earl, and he grew up to be a wealthy nobleman and the ancestor of all future jarls.

With the three classes of Viking society thus created, Rig took on the form of Heimdall once more and went back to where he came from and continued to guard the other gods and goddesses from their enemies.

The Vikings believed that there were nine different realms, arranged on three levels. At the top were Asgard and Vanaheim, homes of the gods and goddesses, and Alheim, home of the helpful Light Elves. In the middle came Midgard where humans lived, Utgard, home of the Giants, Nidavellir, home of the Dwarfs, and Svartalfheim, home of the mischevious Dark Elves. At the bottom were the miserable worlds of Niflheim and Muspell. The Nine Realms were held in place by the roots of the giant ash tree, Yggdrasil. Asgard and Midgard were also joined by a narrow bridge, called Bifrost. It was guarded by Heimdall, one of the Vanir gods.

Viking Society

Viking society was divided into three groups. At the top were the jarls or earls. Then came the karls or freemen, with the thralls or slaves at the bottom. But at first there were no real rulers. Instead, the local Thing or council laid down the rules and settled any arguments. In Norway, Denmark, and Sweden, however, some jarls gradually became more powerful than others. These powerful jarls were often known as kings, but at first each one only ruled over quite a small area. When kings started to rule whole countries, the Things became less important.

The Thing
The Vikings in Iceland were never ruled by kings. Instead they had several local Things and the more powerful Althing which met at Thingvellir for two weeks every summer. All free men could attend and vote on the laws which were recited from the Law Rock.

Viking laws
The laws of the Icelandic Vikings were written down in a book called the Jonsbok.

THE HAVAMAL
As well as looking to their Things for advice, the Vikings could also be guided by the Havamal, a collection of wise sayings which are supposed to have come from Odin himself. They include: praise no day until evening, no wife until buried, no sword until tested, no ice until crossed, no ale until drunk; confide in one, never in two – confide in three and the whole world knows; never part with your weapons when out in the fields – you never know when you will need your spear; and there is no better load a man can carry than much common sense – no worse load than too much drink.

Jarls and slaves
Early Viking society was not rigid. Anyone powerful enough to be a leader or to defeat his rivals could become a jarl, giving other people food and shelter in return for doing heavy work. Most slaves were people who had been captured in raids.

Women

Most Viking women were treated better than women in other parts of Europe at that time. They could own and inherit property whether they were married or single and they were allowed to marry whoever they wanted. They could also get divorced for many different reasons. For example, some women got divorced because their husbands treated them badly, but one divorced her husband because she felt his shirt showed too much of his bare chest! In the home, the wife held the keys to all the storage chests and, if her husband was away, she took charge of the farm and did business on his behalf. She could also intervene in his affairs to keep him out of trouble.

Punishment

Occasionally Vikings were hanged for committing crimes, but more often they had to make a payment to their victim or his family. Those who would not obey the law of the Thing could be sent into exile and, if they refused to go, they could be killed.

The Flateyarbok

The stories of many of the Viking kings of Norway were gathered together in a huge manuscript known as the Flateyarbok. Produced in Iceland around 1390, many of its pages are decorated with beautifully painted pictures representing the kings and their adventures.

Kings and nobility

By the start of the 10th century Denmark, Norway, and Sweden were ruled by kings. Each king hoped to pass on the crown to one of his sons when he died, so making his family into the ruling dynasty. To be able to do this, however, each king needed the support of the jarls who made up the nobility. If the jarls did not approve of the new king, they could overthrow him and put someone else in his place. But some Vikings did not approve of kings at all and many of them went to live in Iceland at this time.

THOR AND JORMUNGAND

Thor, god of Thunder, had vowed to slay the hideous serpent Jormungand. During one of his many voyages he was staying with the giant Hymir. One morning, as Hymir prepared his tackle for the day's fishing, Thor asked to go out to sea with him. Hymir agreed, and Thor rowed out vigorously to where the giant usually fished. Hymir asked Thor to stop, but the god kept rowing. He took them to where the serpent Jormungand lay with its awful coils twisted about the earth.

Thor baited his hook with a bull's head and cast it far out over the waters. The serpent appeared almost immediately, took the gruesome bait in its mouth and swallowed it greedily. When it felt the hook pricking its throat it began to thrash about wildly. It tugged so fiercely that Thor's fists were smashed against the boat's gunwhales. Thor strained so hard against the line that the bottom of the boat gave way beneath him and his feet plunged down until they lodged in the seabed. With his boots thus firmly grounded, he began to haul the serpent toward the boat. He fixed the crazed animal with such a look as would freeze a mortal's blood, while the serpent's fiery gaze spat poisoned arrows back at him. Just as Thor reached for his mighty hammer to

deliver the fatal blow, the terrified Hymir bent forward and quickly cut the line with his fishing knife.

The monster fell back into the sea and vanished into the blue depths. Disgusted by his companion's cowardice, Thor dealt him a fierce blow with his hammer and then set off toward the shore, striding across the bottom of the sea. Thor and Jormungand would meet again, during

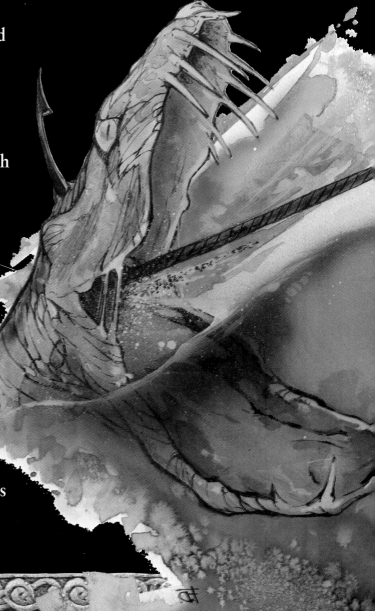

the Twilight of the Gods. On that
occasion Thor would succeed in
defeating his enemy, although it would
cost him his life.

Vikings at Sea

The Viking Age was made possible because of the Vikings' superb shipbuilding and seafaring skills. The Vikings became great sailors because they lived within easy reach of the sea and the rugged geography of their homelands made overland travel difficult. An increase in population in the 8th century led to a shortage of good farming land in Norway, Denmark, and Sweden, and many Vikings began to look to the sea as another way of making a living. At first they went overseas as raiders, attacking towns and monasteries and stealing their treasures, but later they went as traders and settlers, traveling further than any other Europeans at that time.

A picture from 1100 showing Viking raiders about to attack Angers in France in the 9th century.

Overlapping shields protected the rowers.

A weather vane (below) on the ship's prow showed the direction of the wind, so the helmsman could keep the sails at the best angle to the wind.

On the open sea the Vikings used wooden bearing-dials, or sun compasses, with 32 points, to know in which direction they were sailing.

Strong, light, and fast
Viking longships were flexible enough to sail in rough seas without breaking up. They could also sail in very shallow water and land on a beach without damage if there was no harbor. This was useful when the Vikings went raiding as it meant they could land wherever they wanted to, often without being seen until it was too late. The ships were also light enough to be lifted out of the water and carried around obstacles, such as waterfalls and rapids, when the Vikings were sailing on rivers.

BUILDING A VIKING SHIP
Vikings built their ships in winter when it was too cold to work on their farms. Using wood they had cut earlier in the year, they first put the keel in place and supported it on wooden stocks. The front and back posts were then fastened onto it with iron nails. Wedge-shaped planks were then cut for the sides and fastened to the keel from the bottom upward, overlapping each other. After this, wooden ribs were nailed to the planks to keep the ship in shape. Finally the mastblock or keelson, the mast and the rudder were added, along with the sail, the rigging, and the oars.

Trading ships and vessels built to take settlers overseas (right) were heavier and broader than longships. Trading ships also had a half-deck for storing cargo.

Longships (below) were narrower and lighter than trading ships.

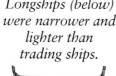

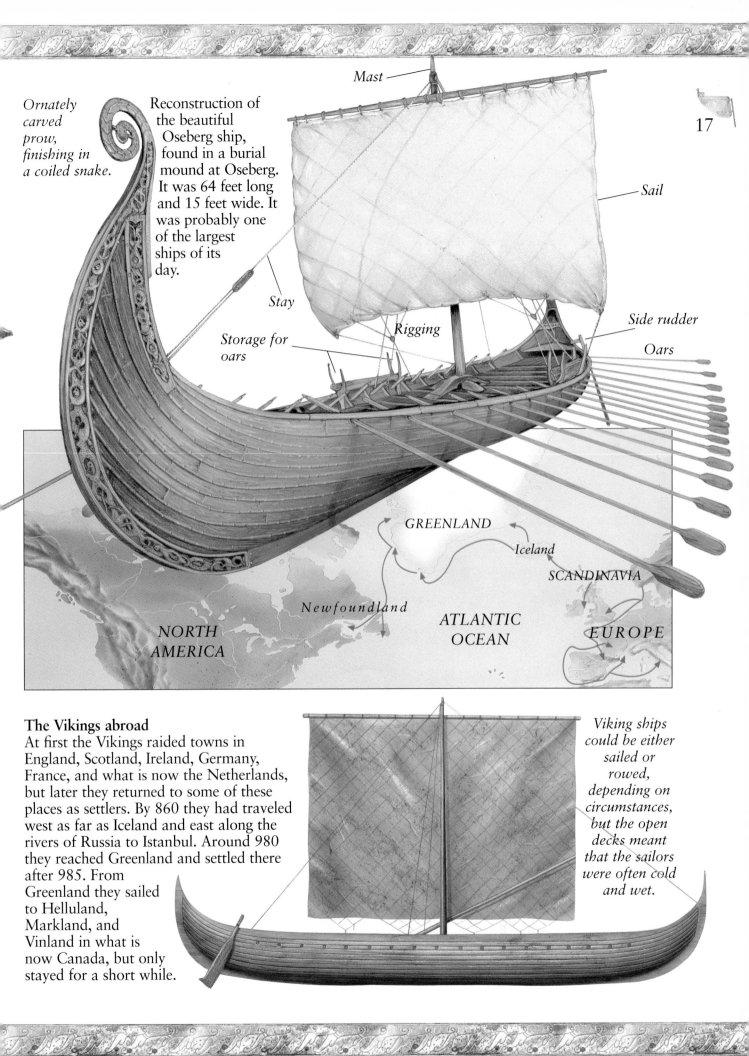

Mast

Sail

Side rudder

Oars

Rigging

Stay

Storage for oars

Ornately carved prow, finishing in a coiled snake.

Reconstruction of the beautiful Oseberg ship, found in a burial mound at Oseberg. It was 64 feet long and 15 feet wide. It was probably one of the largest ships of its day.

GREENLAND

Iceland

SCANDINAVIA

Newfoundland

ATLANTIC OCEAN

EUROPE

NORTH AMERICA

The Vikings abroad

At first the Vikings raided towns in England, Scotland, Ireland, Germany, France, and what is now the Netherlands, but later they returned to some of these places as settlers. By 860 they had traveled west as far as Iceland and east along the rivers of Russia to Istanbul. Around 980 they reached Greenland and settled there after 985. From Greenland they sailed to Helluland, Markland, and Vinland in what is now Canada, but only stayed for a short while.

Viking ships could be either sailed or rowed, depending on circumstances, but the open decks meant that the sailors were often cold and wet.

FREYJA AND THE DWARFS

Freyja was the Viking goddess of love and beauty. She had been married to Odin and, when he left her and disappeared without a trace, she wept tears of gold. She was very beautiful, however, and both men and gods wanted to marry her. She granted her favors to many and brought good harvests and healthy babies to the Viking farmers and their wives. Some of the Dwarfs and Giants also wanted to marry her, but Freyja thought they were not worthy of her attention.

As well as being beautiful herself, Freyja liked beautiful objects, especially jewelry, and this sometimes led her into trouble. Her worst problems came when she wanted a wonderful gold necklace called Brisingamen. It had been made by the Dwarfs, who were skilled metalworkers but were also very cunning. She tried to buy it from them, but the price they asked was that she must spend a night each with four of them in turn. Freyja wanted Brisingamen so much that she agreed to do this.

When the mischievous Loki found out, he told Odin who commanded him to take Brisingamen from Freyja as a punishment for what she had done. Knowing that Freyja liked Brisingamen so much that she even wore it when she was asleep, Loki changed himself into a fly and flew into her bedchamber. He then changed into a flea and bit her on the cheek. This made her turn over in her sleep and Loki was able to unfasten the clasp which held Brisingamen and steal the necklace from around her neck without waking her.

When Freyja realized Brisingamen was missing, she guessed Odin was involved and went to him to demand its return. He agreed to give it back to her, but in return she had to cause wars between kings on earth. She also had to become a goddess of death, choosing half of the bravest warriors as she flew over the battlefields in her chariot which was pulled by two cats.

Clothes and Jewels

Viking clothing was practical rather than stylish and so it changed very little throughout the Viking Age. Most of the garments were made from wool or linen cloth which had been spun from yarn and then woven into cloth by the women in their own homes. Shoes and boots were also usually made at home, using leather from animals which had been killed for food. Some simple jewelry was probably made at home, too, but the best was made by specialist craftworkers in the market towns. Brooches and pins were worn both by men and by women, partly for decoration, partly to show off their wealth, but mainly to fasten their clothes together as they did not have buttons or zips.

Belts and straps
Vikings put decorated metal ends on belts and straps to stop them becoming mis-shapen and to make them easier to fasten.

Viking men often wore armrings made from gold or silver to show how wealthy they were. They could also be used to buy goods.

Women's clothes
Viking women wore a long pleated shift of linen or fine wool under a simple tunic, fastened on the chest with two large brooches. They had no pockets and so items such as keys, a needle-case, and a knife were kept on chains hanging from one of the brooches.

This necklace made from rock crystal and silver would have belonged to a very rich Viking woman.

Glass beads
Most necklaces were made from glass beads in many different colors, shapes, and sizes. The beads themselves were often patterned with different colors of glass. Pendants made from gold or silver coins and other trinkets were sometimes added between the glass beads. Amber, jet, and carnelian were also made into beads.

MAKING FINE JEWELRY

Vikings made fine jewelry in gold or silver by the lost-wax method. First they took a piece of wax and made it into an exact model of the piece of jewelry they wanted to make. They then placed the wax model between two pieces of soft clay to make a mold. They left a hole at the top and several small holes at the bottom. When the clay had hardened, they poured molten gold or silver into the hole at the top. This melted the wax which ran out at the bottom, while the molten metal took its place. When the metal had cooled and set solid, the mold was broken and the piece of jewelry taken out.

Men's clothes

Viking men wore tight-fitting trousers and a long-sleeved tunic with a belt at the waist. In cold weather they also wore a cloak, fastened with a brooch on one shoulder to keep their sword-arm free in case of a fight.

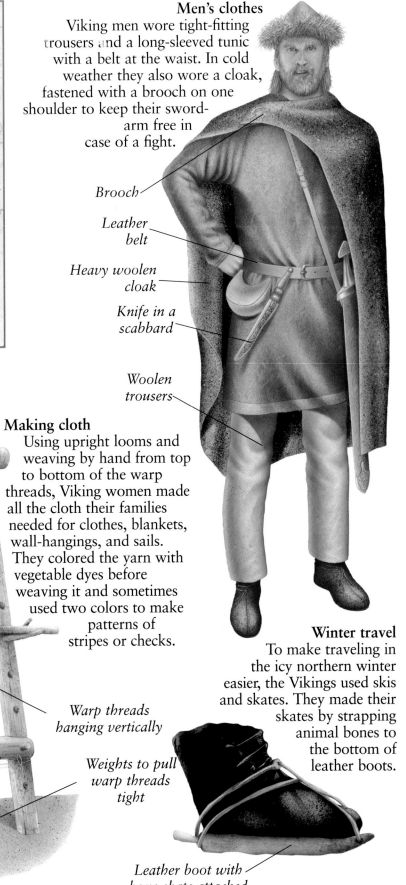

Brooch

Leather belt

Heavy woolen cloak

Knife in a scabbard

Woolen trousers

Making cloth

Using upright looms and weaving by hand from top to bottom of the warp threads, Viking women made all the cloth their families needed for clothes, blankets, wall-hangings, and sails. They colored the yarn with vegetable dyes before weaving it and sometimes used two colors to make patterns of stripes or checks.

Beam to separate warp threads

Warp threads hanging vertically

Weights to pull warp threads tight

Winter travel

To make traveling in the icy northern winter easier, the Vikings used skis and skates. They made their skates by strapping animal bones to the bottom of leather boots.

Leather boot with bone skate attached

AEGIR'S FEAST

L oki lived in Asgard and was treated as one of the gods, even though he was the son of two Fire Giants. In his youth, he loved adventures, mystery, and disguise. He also amused the gods with his mischief and trickery. Sometimes he was deceitful, however, and told lies about other people to get them into trouble. Eventually the gods began to tire of his behavior and wanted little to do with him. This made Loki very bitter and instead of being mischievous, he became spiteful and evil.

In this new mood Loki grew jealous of Balder. He was Odin's son and was loved by everyone for his kindness and his wisdom. He lived happily with his wife, Nanna, and brought peace and harmony wherever he went. But Loki used trickery to kill Balder, then prevented him from returning to life by refusing to weep for him. The gods were heartbroken over Balder's death. Their mourning lasted for a very long time, during which Loki avoided their company. Then Aegir, the sea god, and his wife, Ran, decided everyone had been sad for long enough. They organized a great feast in their underwater hall and invited all the gods and goddesses to it to cheer them up. Loki was the only one not to be invited, but he was determined to go.

Using trickery again, he appeared in Aegir's hall when the feast was well under way and the gods had started to be happy again.

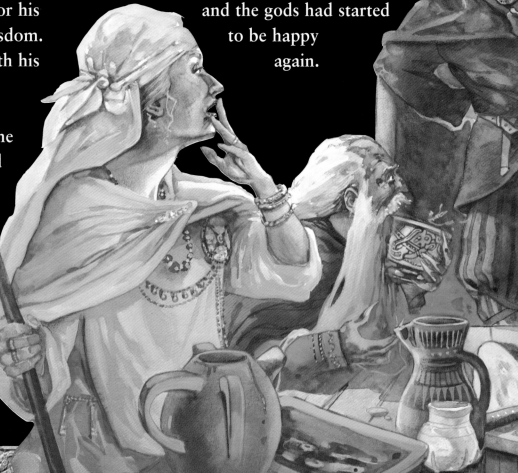

This angered Loki so much that he made a speech insulting each of them and telling all their secrets. He then tried to flee from the hall, but the gods chased after him. To get away, he disguised himself as a salmon and leapt into a waterfall. He could no longer fool the gods, however, and they quickly got a net to catch him. They decided he should suffer for what he had done and so they took him to a cave in the mountains and tied him across sharp rocks. Then they placed a poisonous snake above his head so that venom from its fangs would drip onto his face and cause him great pain. Only his wife felt sorry for him and she held a bowl to catch the poison. But whenever she had to empty it, the poison fell on Loki's face again and he would writhe in agony until she returned.

Food and Entertainment

The Vikings usually ate two main meals each day, one in the morning after a few hours' work, and one in the evening at nightfall. Food was served in wooden bowls or on wooden plates and was eaten with fingers, knives, or spoons (there were no forks). The main drinks were buttermilk and beer, but mead and wine were drunk on special occasions. These included three festivals each year. They were Sigrblot at the start of summer, Vetrarblot just after the harvest, and Jolablot just after midwinter.

Only rich people drank wine, which was imported from the south. This pottery wine jug was probably brought back from Germany.

Fish
Fish played an important part in the Vikings' diet. If it was not eaten fresh, it could be preserved by gutting it, then smoking it over the fire, treating it with salt, or hanging it up in the sun to dry.

Metal hoops

Cooking food
Food was cooked indoors. Porridge and stews could be prepared in a cauldron hanging from a tripod over the fire. Meat was also roasted on spits, while fish could be placed between two layers of grass and baked between red-hot stones.

Storing food
Containers for dry food or liquids were made from vertical wooden staves bound tightly together with horizontal metal hoops. The very ornate container (above) obviously comes from a wealthy Viking household.

Metal cauldron

Leg of iron tripod

Entertainment

In summer the Vikings enjoyed swimming, rowing, and sailing, as well as competitions for running, jumping, fencing, archery, and weight-lifting. They also played ball-games and enjoyed wrestling and horse-racing, and betting on the results. In winter they skated over frozen rivers and lakes. When it was too cold outside, they made music and played games inside.

This carving from a rune-stone shows two men playing a board game. It could be hnefitafl, *which was a Viking invention, but no rules have survived to tell us how it was played.*

King

Queen

Viking traders probably brought chess back from Arabia. These pieces were carved from walrus ivory.

Bishops

Finger holes for different notes

This bone flute from Sweden is one of the few musical instruments to survive from Viking times. It was played like a modern recorder.

A VIKING BANQUET

On special occasions, such as a wedding or a religious festival, the Vikings celebrated with a special meal. Everyone wore their best clothes and linen cloths were spread over the tables. In the wealthiest households, imported wine was served in small silver cups, but most people would drink mead or beer from drinking horns. These were made from the horns of cattle and were often decorated with bands of gold or silver. The meal would include horsemeat, beef or pork served on a fine silver dish, and perhaps game such as venison or hare. After the meal, the guests were entertained with music, singing, and dancing, as well as poetry and storytelling.

The Vikings added to their diet by hunting. As the carving on this stone (right) shows, they used hawks and falcons to hunt and kill other wild birds and small animals, which were brought back by trained dogs.

This hnefitafl board (above) was found in the Irish village of Ballinderry, but was probably made by Vikings in 10th-century Dublin. Similar boards found in Gokstad and York have more than twice as many pegholes.

THE VALKYRIES

Asgard, the home of the Aesir gods, was divided into many different halls. The most magnificent was Valhalla, which belonged to Odin. Its roof was made from golden spears and its walls were lined with golden shields. The name meant the Hall of the Slain and it was the final home of Viking warriors and kings who had been killed in battle. Half of these warriors were chosen by the goddess Freyja. The rest were chosen by the Valkyries, Odin's maidservants who sometimes dressed like warriors themselves. They had names such as Battle, Shrieking, and Shaker and often swooped over a battle on their horses to direct the fighting and make sure that the warriors they had chosen were killed.

Once the warriors were dead, the Valkyries picked them up and transported them to Valhalla. They usually went one by one on horseback, but if the Valkyries had chosen a lot of warriors or the battle had been near the sea, they could go by boat instead. As they reached Valhalla, other Valkyries came out to meet them, carrying golden drinking horns filled with mead or beer. The warriors were restored to life and their wounds were swiftly healed as they were welcomed into Odin's hall. There a great feast of roast boar was set out for them and they could sit at the table and eat their fill, waited on by the Valkyries and surrounded by the other warriors who had died before them. They told tales of their adventures and of the battles they had been in. And, as the night went on, they laughed and sang and got happily drunk, before going to their beds to sleep.

When they woke next morning, they were refreshed and ready for battle again. They put on their helmets and picked up their swords, spears, battle-axes, and shields. Then they went to a special battleground where they could fight against each other all day. They could be wounded or even killed there, but in the evening they all returned to Valhalla where the wounded were healed and the dead restored to life once more. The Valkyries had another great feast waiting for them in the hall and once more the warriors ate and drank, told tales, laughed and sang throughout the evening. Then they went to bed and rested, ready for the daily round of fighting and feasting to begin again.

War and Warriors

The Vikings were fierce and fearless warriors. Within Scandinavia chieftains fought to gain control of large, rich kingdoms. Then, from about 800 onward, they began to raid England, Ireland, and other European countries. At first the raids were carried out by small bands who plundered coastal villages and then returned home with their booty. Before long, however, well-organized war parties were being sent by kings to invade, plunder, and seize land. By 845 their reputation was so powerful that they were able to persuade the king of Paris to give them 6600 pounds of silver to leave his city in peace. This payment was known as Danegeld and, over the next 200 years, vast amounts of it were paid to various Viking armies, especially by the kings of England.

The carving on this gravestone at Middleton-on-the-Wolds, England, shows a Viking warrior and his weapons. His sword and his battleaxe are on his left and his shield is shown above them.

Helmets

Viking warriors wore close-fitting iron helmets in battle. Many had long guards to protect the wearer's nose and cheeks, which must have made the warriors look very frightening.

Swords

A Viking sword was used to slash at the enemy, rather than stab him. Its blade was made from several rods of iron, twisted together when hot and then hammered flat. This made it flexible enough not to break in battle. The cutting edges were made of better quality iron and were welded on. The hilt, or handle, was also made of iron and often decorated with gold or silver.

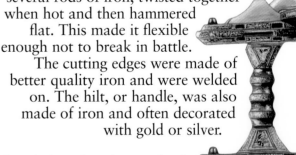

Viking helmet found in England and dating from before the first Viking raids. It shows that Scandinavia and England were in contact from earliest times.

THE VIKING KINGS OF ENGLAND

In 1016 an army of Danish Vikings led by their king, Svein Forkbeard, defeated the English army at the battle of Ashingdon. Svein then became king of England as well as king of Denmark. He died that year and was succeeded by his son, Cnut. In 1030 Cnut and his army defeated Olaf Haraldsson, king of Norway, at the battle of Stiklarstad. Cnut then ruled Norway, as well as Denmark and England. After Cnut's death in 1035, his son Hardacnut succeeded him. When he died in 1042, an Englishman, Edward the Confessor, became the next king.

Dagger

Arrows

Arrow

Bow

Leather quiver

Battle

At the start of a pitched battle, the Vikings fired arrows and then threw spears at their enemies before the hand-to-hand fighting started. They used swords, axes, and daggers. Those who could afford them, protected their bodies with chain-mail shirts.

Helmet

Chain-mail shirt

Battle-axe

Shield

Sword

Strips of leather to protect the legs

Fortresses

The sites of five possible Viking fortresses have been found in Denmark. They all date from the late 10th century and have a similar layout. They may have been barracks for soldiers, but archeological evidence shows that women and children also lived and died there, and some of the buildings were workshops for blacksmiths and jewelers.

Housing

Circular rampart

Street

Each fortress was protected by a circular rampart and divided into four equal segments by two streets which crossed at the center.

Weapons

Viking warriors sometimes rode on horseback to the site of a battle, but they always fought on foot. They provided their own weapons and the best were passed down from one generation to the next. Their shields were made of wood, with an iron boss in the middle. This could also be used as a weapon if the rest of the shield was destroyed.

THE VANIR GODS

The gods of the Vanir family were the guardians of pastures and forests, rain and sunlight. They brought peace and good harvests to the land and controlled storms at sea. Originally they had all lived in Vanaheim and had been enemies of the Aesir gods. When the two families made peace with each other the three most important Vanir gods went to live in Asgard. They were Njord, the main sea god, and his children Frey and Freyja. Njord's wife was a Mountain Giantess called Skadi. But their marriage was unhappy because she loved the mountains and Njord loved the sea. Eventually they agreed to live apart and their children lived with Njord.

In spite of his father's unhappy experience, Frey also wanted to marry a Giantess whose name was Gerd. He had spied her one day when he had broken the rules of Asgard by sneaking into Odin's hall and sitting on Odin's throne. From there he could see into Jotunheim, the land of the Frost Giants, where the beautiful Gerd lived with her family. Frey fell headlong in love with her and soon could not eat or sleep for thinking about her. This was a punishment from Odin for daring to sit on his throne, but when Njord learnt what had happened, he decided to help Frey.

It was too dangerous to send Frey himself to Jotunheim and so Njord sent his servant Skirnir to woo Gerd on Frey's behalf. Skirnir took with him Frey's magic sword, which could move through the air by itself, and his magic horse, which could see in the dark and gallop through the icy flames which surrounded Gerd's home. When he reached Gerd, Skirnir offered her wealth and the golden apples of eternal youth, as well as Frey's love. But her heart was made of ice and she rejected him. Exasperated by her reaction, Skirnir finally threatened to kill her father, Gymir. At that she promised to meet Frey in nine days' time.

Skirnir hurried back to tell him and, to Frey's delight, Gerd kept her promise. When they met, Frey's love melted the ice in Gerd's heart and she became warm and loving. Their marriage was thought to symbolize the sun melting the ice in springtime and allowing the earth to become warm and produce crops again.

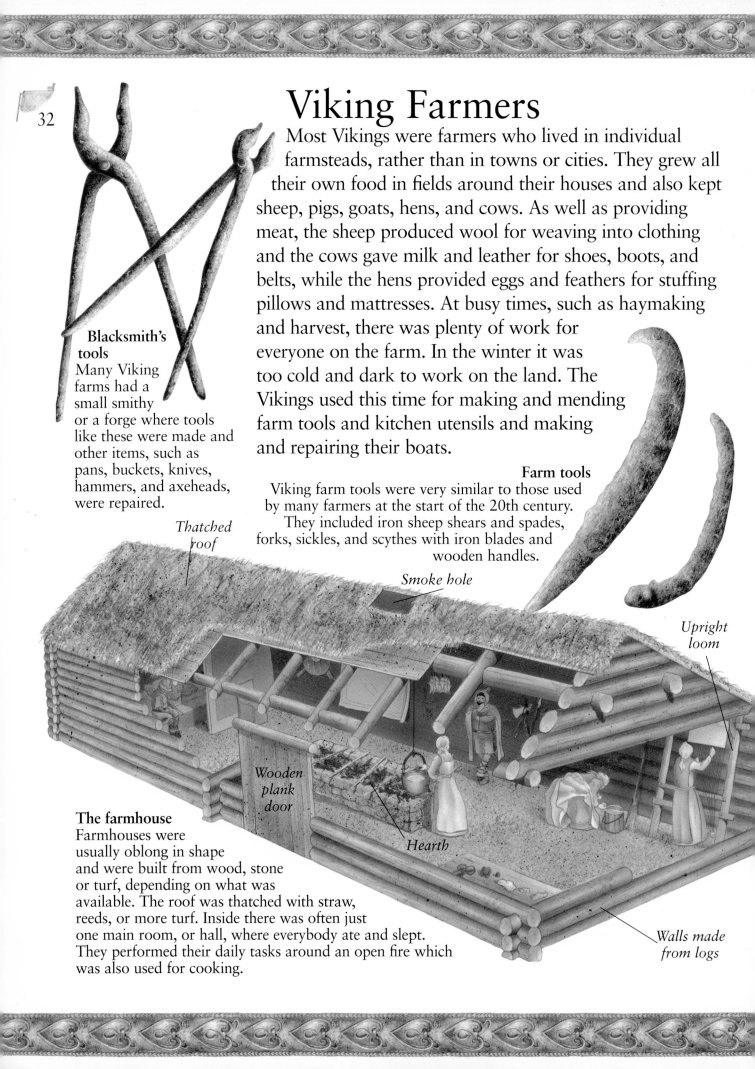

Viking Farmers

Most Vikings were farmers who lived in individual farmsteads, rather than in towns or cities. They grew all their own food in fields around their houses and also kept sheep, pigs, goats, hens, and cows. As well as providing meat, the sheep produced wool for weaving into clothing and the cows gave milk and leather for shoes, boots, and belts, while the hens provided eggs and feathers for stuffing pillows and mattresses. At busy times, such as haymaking and harvest, there was plenty of work for everyone on the farm. In the winter it was too cold and dark to work on the land. The Vikings used this time for making and mending farm tools and kitchen utensils and making and repairing their boats.

Blacksmith's tools
Many Viking farms had a small smithy or a forge where tools like these were made and other items, such as pans, buckets, knives, hammers, and axeheads, were repaired.

Farm tools
Viking farm tools were very similar to those used by many farmers at the start of the 20th century. They included iron sheep shears and spades, forks, sickles, and scythes with iron blades and wooden handles.

Thatched roof

Smoke hole

Upright loom

Wooden plank door

Hearth

Walls made from logs

The farmhouse
Farmhouses were usually oblong in shape and were built from wood, stone or turf, depending on what was available. The roof was thatched with straw, reeds, or more turf. Inside there was often just one main room, or hall, where everybody ate and slept. They performed their daily tasks around an open fire which was also used for cooking.

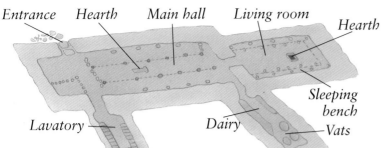

Entrance   Hearth   Main hall   Living room

Hearth

Sleeping bench

Lavatory   Dairy   Vats

The farm at Stöng

This plan is of a Viking farmhouse at Stöng in Iceland. It was abandoned around 1104 when a volcanic eruption covered the surrounding land in ash. Archeologists excavated the site in 1939 and, using the evidence they found, built a full-scale reconstruction of the house nearby. The walls and roof were made from turf and there were three rooms besides the hall.

GROWING GRAIN

In the northern Viking lands, the main grain crops were barley, oats, and rye. In the south, where it was warmer, they could also grow wheat. Before the seeds were planted in spring, the fields were spread with animal manure which had been collected in the farmyard over the winter. The manure acted as a fertilizer to make the plants grow well. There were no pesticides and so all the weeds had to be pulled out by hand. The grain from each harvest was used to make porridge, bread, and soups, and to brew beer. Some was kept as seed for the following year.

Viking crops

As well as growing grain crops in the fields, the Vikings grew fruit, herbs, and vegetables around their houses. Where it was warm enough, they had apple and plum trees and also grew strawberries and raspberries. In most places they could also grow carrots, onions, leeks, peas, beans, and cabbages, as well as garlic and mint to flavor their food.

The Vikings needed all the grass that grew in the meadows around the farmstead to make into hay to feed the animals they kept over the winter. When the weather started to warm up in the spring, the sheep and cattle were taken up into the hills for the summer to feed on the grass there.

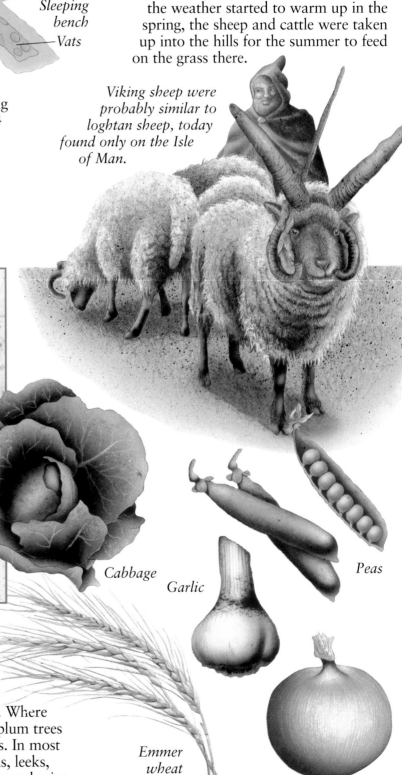

Viking sheep were probably similar to loghtan sheep, today found only on the Isle of Man.

Cabbage

Garlic

Peas

Emmer wheat

Onion

ODIN STEALS THE MEAD OF POETRY

When the Aesir and Vanir gods made peace with each other after their quarrel, they sealed their agreement by all spitting into a huge jar. From this spittle a large man, called Kvasir, was formed. Although he was as big as a Giant, he was gentle. He was also very wise as he had inherited wisdom from each of the gods.

Unfortunately, two of the Dwarfs were jealous of his wisdom and wanted to steal it for themselves. They invited Kvasir to a feast and then murdered him. His blood filled three cauldrons and the Dwarfs mixed it with honey to make a special mead. Anyone who drank it would be inspired to write poetry, which was a gift that the Vikings valued very highly.

Knowing this mead was very precious, the Dwarfs guarded it carefully. One day, however, they made the mistake of murdering one of the relations of the Giant Suttungr. He went to the Dwarfs, intending to kill them in vengeance for the murder, but when they offered him the mead, he took that instead and spared their lives. Suttungr then hid the three cauldrons of mead deep inside a mountain and set his daughter, Gunnlod to guard them. But he could not resist boasting about what had happened and, when the gods heard about it, they decided they wanted the mead for themselves. Disguised as a handsome Giant by the name of Bolverk, Odin caused a quarrel between the nine men who worked for Suttungr's brother, Baugi. When the men had killed each other, Odin offered to take their place for the summer, asking only for a drink of mead as his wages. Baugi agreed, but at the end of the summer Suttungr refused to allow Odin his drink. Angry, Odin forced Baugi to tell him where the mead was hidden and, turning himself into a snake, sneaked inside the mountain through a tiny hole. Turning himself back into the handsome Bolverk, he started flattering Gunnlod. She soon fell in love with him and, after three nights, was persuaded to give him three sips of the mead. With each sip, Odin emptied a cauldron. He then turned himself into an eagle and flew back to Asgard, where the gods had three new cauldrons waiting for him. Odin spat one-third of the mead into each and later used it to give the gift of poetry to specially chosen humans.

Writing and Literature

The Vikings were great storytellers and many of their stories, or "sagas", and histories can still be read today. In Viking times they were learnt by heart and handed down from one generation to the next by word of mouth. Few Vikings had the opportunity to learn to read and write the "runes" (Viking letters). Some of them knew how to write their name on a sword or a comb, but there were no schools and they did not have pens or paper, or even use parchment like other people in Europe did at that time. If any sort of formal writing was needed, it was done by skilled men, known as rune-masters, who could carve the words into stone, bone, metal or wood.

Many of the Vikings' sagas were first written down in the 13th century. They were written on vellum (made of calfskin) and bound in wooden covers (top).

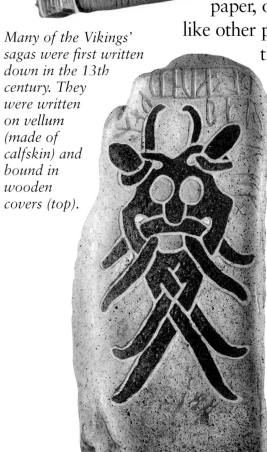

A mask carved on a rune-stone and then painted (above). It was probably intended to frighten away evil spirits.

A 17th-century picture of Egil Skallagrimsson, the hero of Egil's Saga. An adventurer and poet, he was born in Norway, but spent much of his life in exile in Iceland.

Words and pictures

Many rune-stones were carved with pictures as well as with words. Favorite subjects included scenes from Viking myths and images of mythical creatures, such as dragons and huge serpents. These creatures were often shown as a tangle of legs and bodies, twisting in and out of each other and earning them the name of Gripping Beasts. After carving, the images were often painted in bold colors, with red, black, and yellow being the most popular. The carvings of the runes themselves were also often painted in red, as on this stone (left) from Arhus in Denmark. They tell us that, "Gunulv and Ogot and Aslak and Rolf set up this stone in memory of Ful, their partner. He met his death...when kings fought."

Carving runes onto stone was a skilled job and took a lot of time and patience.

The Vikings believed that Odin gave one of his eyes and hung from a branch of Yggdrasil for nine days and nights to gain knowledge of the runes and pass it on to humans. Because of this, they were first thought to be magical, giving strength to swords and stopping items from getting lost. Later they were carved onto rune-stones in memory of dead Vikings. In the Viking homelands these stones often commemorate Vikings who died overseas, giving us clues as to how far they traveled.

The longest known Viking inscription is on the Rökstone in Ostergötland, Sweden. A man called Varin put it up in memory of his son, Vaermad.

VIKING POETRY

The Vikings were fond of poetry and it was often an important part of the entertainment at a feast. After the meal, the poet or skald, was asked to recite old poems or even to make up some new ones. Some described past adventures and battles, but others were made up of verses, known as "drapa", in praise of the host of the feast. According to legend, the best poets could save their lives if they were ever captured by their enemies by composing a poem praising their enemy's leader who, flattered, would set them free.

The futhark

The futhark was the Viking equivalent of our alphabet. Its name comes from its first six letters, or runes, which were f, u, th, a, r, and k. Runes were all made up of straight lines to make it easier to carve them into hard objects, such as memorial stones. There were two slightly different versions of the futhark, but each one had only 16 letters. This meant that there were not enough symbols for all the sounds in the language, making it difficult for a rune-master to decide how to spell a word. For example, the futhark had no symbols for the sounds d, g, and p, and so the rune-master used t, k, and b instead. Although there were two symbols for a, there were none for e or o.

Runes were also carved onto everyday objects, such as combs. The piece of wood (bottom) is a medieval calendar, carved with runes.

f u th a r k   h n i a   s t b m l R

THE TWILIGHT OF THE GODS

The Vikings believed that their gods would eventually be killed in a fierce battle against the Giants. Before this happened, however, there would be war among humans and Midgard itself would freeze over. The only people to escape death at this time would be a man and a woman, called Lif and Lifthrasir, who would shelter in the branches of Yggdrasil. The sun and the moon would then be swallowed by the huge wolves, Skoll and Hati, who had been chasing them across the skies since the creation of the world. The stars would go out and Midgard would plunge into darkness.

The wicked Loki would escape from the cave where he had been imprisoned after Aegir's feast and join forces with the wolf, Fenrir. They would then join up with the Giants and the fiery beings from Muspell to attack Asgard. The rainbow bridge, Bifrost, would be destroyed and all the monsters would escape, but Heimdall, the guardian of Bifrost, would survive to warn the Nine Realms of the forthcoming battle, known as Ragnarok.

This battle world take place on a great plain, known as Vigard, and here the gods and their enemies would fight to the death. Odin would be accompanied by his sons and all the dead Vikings from Valhalla. In spite of this great army of experienced warriors, however, he would be killed and eaten by Fenrir. Odin's son, Vidar, would then kill Fenrir while Loki and Heimdall killed each other. Jormungand, the giant sea serpent, would come out of the sea and attack Thor who would kill him, but die of his poison.

After the battle, Surt, the guardian of Muspell, would destroy Asgard and Midgard by fire and the Nine Realms would sink into the sea. At first it would seem that only Yggdrasil had survived, but slowly land would rise from the sea, and the sun's daughter would come to warm the new earth. Plants and animals would reappear and Lif and Lifthrasir would come down from the branches of Yggdrasil to start the human race again.

Trade and Transport

The Vikings' superb ships and sailing skills, plus their adventurous natures, allowed them to set up trade links with almost all of the world as it was then known. As well as trading among themselves, Vikings from Norway and Denmark traded with people in western Europe, Iceland, and Greenland, while Vikings from Sweden sailed east across the Baltic and along the rivers of Russia to the great markets of Turkey and the Middle East. There they met Arab traders from whom they bought silk from China and spices, such as pepper, cloves, and ginger, to flavor their food. These goods were then traded on in the main Viking market towns of Birka in Sweden, Hedeby in Denmark, and Kaupang in Norway.

Charms for safety
This small statue is thought to represent Thor with his magic hammer, Mjollnir. Many Vikings believed that it would also help to protect them from Dwarfs and other threats, especially when they had to travel over mountains or in rocky places which they thought were dangerous. They had small replicas made of it, often in silver, and wore them as lucky charms or amulets.

This bronze statue of Buddha from northern India was found in Helgö in Sweden. It shows just how extensive the Vikings' trade links were.

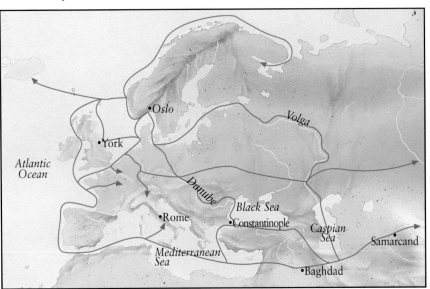

Trade routes
The map shows the Vikings' main trade routes by sea, river, and land. They used the Russian rivers to reach the Black Sea and the Caspian Sea. From the Black Sea they sailed to Constantinople (modern Istanbul), but to get to Baghdad they had to leave their ships on the shores of the Caspian Sea and travel the rest of the way by camel.

There were very few roads in the Vikings' lands, so people traveled by water whenever they could. If they had to go any distance overland, they either walked or went on horseback. However, they used wagons and carts to move goods around in the towns and on the farms. They also used sledges which could be pulled over grass or ice and snow, depending on the time of year.

Carved runner

The sledge (above) and the four-wheeled wagon (right) were found in the Oseberg ship burial. They were both pulled by horses, but with their carved panels they were far more ornate than those in everyday use.

Buying and selling

For most of the Viking Age the Scandinavian traders did not use coins to pay for the goods they bought. The first Danish coins were minted early in the 9th century but they were not widely used until about 1000. Instead of using money, the traders exchanged their goods for something of equal or greater value, or for a weight of silver or gold. This could be in the form of weights, small bars, or pieces of jewelry. These could be cut up to make the correct weight to buy more goods or melted down to make more jewelry.

Axle

Wooden wheels

LUXURY GOODS

Although Viking ships could travel quickly, they could not carry very large cargoes and so most Vikings traded in luxury goods which did not take up a lot of space but had a high value. From their homelands they took furs, walrus ivory, amber, hides, feathers, ropes, wax, honey, and even live birds of prey, to exchange for silk, brocade, spices, silver, jewelry, wine, glass, pottery, sword-blades, and fruit. They also took people who had been captured in raids and sold them as slaves in the markets at Baghdad and Constantinople.

A portable balance-scale, used for weighing silver.

Small weights like the ones shown here were used with the portable scales. When the Vikings were ruled by kings, coins were minted in their homelands and using coins gradually replaced the system of weighing silver.

End of the Viking World

The Viking Age lasted for around 300 years. There were several reasons why it ended. One was the spread of Christianity to Norway, Denmark, Sweden, and Iceland which made the Vikings change their way of life. Another was an improvement in farming in the Viking homelands which made more land available. This meant that younger sons no longer had to migrate. At around the same time, Vikings who had migrated started marrying into the local populations and began to adopt their ways. Trade also changed and, as bigger ships were needed to carry bulkier goods, the Viking traders became less important in international trade.

The Jelling Stone has both Viking and Christian carvings. It was set up at Jelling, in Denmark, by King Harald Bluetooth, who made his country Christian around 960.

The Bayeux Tapestry is a long piece of medieval embroidery with more than 70 scenes of the Norman Conquest of England.

The Norman Conquest
In 1066 England was conquered by Duke William of Normandy's army. The French-speaking Normans were of Viking descent. Their ancestors had settled in France after 911 when the French king gave them land on condition that they would defend France from attacks by other Vikings.

Vikings in Greenland
The Vikings first settled in Greenland in about 985. Farms were set up and the Vikings appear to have thrived even in the very tough climate. But in the 15th century, the climate cooled and the ice increased. Ships could no longer get through and the settlements were abandoned.

Ships visiting the Viking colonies in Greenland in the 14th century kept the settlers up to date with European fashions, as shown by this hooded cape found there.

The last raids
A new series of raids on England started in 991 when the Vikings won the Battle of Maldon in Essex. To try to keep the peace, the English kings paid out vast amounts of money as Danegeld, but the raids continued until the Norman Conquest.

This staring wooden face gives an idea of the ferocity of the Viking spirit.

RAGNAROK

The Vikings believed that their gods would be destroyed by the Giants in a mighty battle called Ragnarok. Midgard would freeze, killing all but two humans who would hide in Yggdrasil's branches. Two wolves would swallow the sun and the moon. Loki and Fenrir would fight against the gods. Fenrir would kill Odin, then be killed by Odin's son. Thor would kill the serpent Jormungand, but die from its poison, while Loki and Heimdall would kill each other. The Nine Realms would be destroyed, but Yggdrasil and the two humans would survive so life could start anew.

Dragon-headed decorations

Stave churches

43

As they became Christians, the Norwegians built beautiful wooden churches known as stave churches. The church at Borgund on Sogne Fjord in Norway is a fine example of a stave church. Built in the 12th century, its walls are made of tree-trunks, split into two and standing vertically. Its roof is also made of wood. Although a Christian church, it is decorated with Viking dragons' heads, as well as crosses.

Steeply pitched roof

Viking craftworkers

Even after they became Christians, Viking craftspeople kept their own distinct styles, as this gold crucifix shows.

Entrance

The mold (left) from Denmark could be used to make Christian crosses (top) and pagan Thor's hammers (above).

The Viking Age faded, but images of the Vikings remain.

Scandinavia after the Vikings

By 1100 Denmark and Norway were united Christian kingdoms. Paganism remained strong in Sweden for another century, then it too became a Christian monarchy. During the 11th and 12th centuries the Scandinavians were themselves victims of raids from Slavic tribes from the south. By the 13th century the old Viking kingdoms had been replaced by medieval Christian monarchies.

INDEX